GROW ANOTHER GARDEN

Written by Crystal Falk

For Wade Flatt

Dedicated to

_____

_____

_____

_____

_____

_____

_____

"We wished upon a star,
and you came true."

- Unknown

Dedicated with Love

Cambria G. 06/03/11	August L.H. 09/20/13	Aven B. 02/24/08
Chase G. 06/03/11	Hardy B.L. 08/27/15	Felix L. 07/29/14
Jayden M. 07/12/12	Maxwell B. 11/30/16	Jacob M. 03/19/16
Rhys SB 10/2016	Blake A. 03/21/13	Nikki S. 04/2016
Sawyer SB 10/2016	Olivia A. 03/21/13	Lydia K. 06/20/16
Brooks B. 12/31/11	Campbell M. 09/15/14	Grayson H. 03/25/16
Brehn B. 12/31/11	Sailor M. 07/18/16	Kamryn R. 12/29/14
Davin P. 10/13/13	Grayson R. 04/28/15	Luke Z. 07/08/12
Peter P. 10/13/13	Isabelle R. 02/14/11	Mark Z. 07/08/12
Libby W. 02/27/15	Mabel R. 03/16/13	Jack C.
Logan D. 07/01/16	Genevieve R. 03/16/13	Ryusei S. 09/23/10
Collin H. 07/31/14	Mikaela K. 03/04/15	Cooper H-K. 02/11/12
Hannah Lanier H. 07/31/14	Ava F. 02/11/15	Benjamin H. 05/22/15
Monroe M. 02/18/16	James D. 05/14/14	Henry J. 03/24/15
Rowan N. 06/11/15	Victor B. 12/03/10	Mia A. 08/15/16
Lily Diane A.P. 08/30/16	Vincent B. 12/03/10	Shaun S. 02/11/14
Colin L.	William Liam W. 12/12/13	Roman M. 10/2014
Milton L.	Nola W. 12/12/13	Emilia R. 04/2016
Marco T. 05/13/15	Chloe W. 04/03/12	Elena B. 08/23/14
Giuliana T. 05/13/15	Elvis W. 12/12/13	Pablo B. 07/09/16
Espn D.	Emily W. 12/12/13	Lucia B. 07/09/16
Rylan F. 06/16/16	Eila F. 10/10/13	Alicia S. 12/14/15
Madison F. 09/22/14	Abril O. 05/19/15	Valentina S. 12/14/15
Robbyn C. 10/02/15	Pol O. 05/19/15	Dominick D. 05/12/15
Baptist A. 02/23/15	Ava H. 09/2012	Sienna D. 05/12/15
Alice D. 08/04/16	Kiera H. 09/2012	Charlotte S. 11/06/15
Ethan K. 10/24/15	Ridley L. 04/2014	Alyssa C. 10/17/08
Nathan K. 10/24/15	Amaya S. 06/2016	Vanessa C. 10/17/08
Talitha B. 03/20/15	Ian T. 04/28/03	Maxwell M. 05/31/11
Johannes L.H. 09/20/13	Anthony F. 11/02/04	

Miles N. 03/11/13
Grace F. 06/17/15
Maximus E. 03/02/15
Scarlett E. 03/02/15
Deion A. 12/15/15
Dante A. 12/15/15
Charlotte N. 11/16/15
Elizabeth N. 11/16/15
Raúl V.P. 10/13/15
Ben F. 2012
Hannah F. 2012
Hayden A. 2015
Ryder A. 2015
Alexander Roy B. 02/09/16
Madyson C. 02/2016
Taylor C. 02/2016
Declan S. 10/2015
Klara 04/03/14
Ella 12/2014
Ceasar 12/2014
David V. 05/18/16
Olivia V. 05/18/16
Norah O. 02/08/15
Griffin O. 04/06/16
Anna O. 04/06/16
Andrew S. 07/27/16
Ines O.
Alix O.
Danny N. 07/01/16
Blair T. 04/07/2016
Elena R. 07/08/16
Ana R. 07/08/16

Raven B. 04/15/14
Bodhi B. 04/15/14
Paxton L. 01/20/17
Jace H.
Liam R. 05/03/10
Dylan R. 05/03/10
Talma R. 01/25/12
Aviad R. 01/25/12
Mark W. 07/12/16
Carly K. 07/03/16
Richard W. 05/25/16
William W. 05/25/16
Paige L. 06/28/12
Isabella B. 06/27/14
Alex L. 04/21/16
Venice V. 07/15/15
Stephen S. 08/15/16
Ava M. 05/06/14
Owen M. 05/06/14
Lillian L.
Annie N. 08/22/16
Eloise H. 02/2016
Thorben H. 02/2016
Romain H-G. 07/17/15
Kirsa B. 07/28/15
Mamie L. 05/05/16
Sutton C. 03/03/10
Ryan M. 02/09/12
Nicholas M. 07/20/13
Jameson B. 12/22/15
Aman 07/09/12
Nate 07/14/15

Bryson P L. 09/10/15
Yael A. 05/18/16
Hadar A. 05/18/16
Sagi MT. 02/29/16
Shira Esther C.S. 11/2013
Markus R. 06/28/13
Etai B.Y. 06/18/16
Uri R.A. 10/16/15
Stanley F.S. 09/27/16
Caren F.S. 09/27/16
Averi V. 08/2014
Tenli V. 08/2014
Birkli V. 09/2016
Mason B. 08/01/15
Grayson R. 11/2016

"I love you more than the moon and all the stars."

-Grown in Another Garden

Mikey was a little boy who lived in the city

with his mom, dad and his little puppy, Rover.

Mikey was so full of energy! He loved playing outside, running around and splashing in the mud.

Sometimes Rover would splash in the mud too!

Gardening was something Mikey and
his mom liked to do together.

Watermelons were his favorite type of fruit.
His mom and dad loved them too.

They loved how big watermelons could grow and how sweet they tasted. Watermelons are so yummy and special.

"Mom, can we grow a watermelon in our garden?,"
Mikey asked excitedly.

Mikey's mom explained their garden
was way too small to grow watermelons.

"Although our garden is too small, Grandma has a big garden which is perfect for growing watermelons. Let's ask if we can grow some there."

Mikey was very excited! He
loved spending time with his Grandma.

They both loved to spend time together in the garden.

Mikey's grandmother grew different
types of flowers, fruits and vegetables.

"Some types of fruits and vegetables need special places to grow. Some of them also need special care," Grandma explained.

Mikey loved to read and learn about gardening from his grandmother. His favorite type of watermelon was called Moon and Stars Watermelon.

This was his favorite because his mother would always say,
"I love you more than the moon and all the stars." Looking at the
watermelon reminded him of how special he was.

Before Mikey was born, his mom and dad really wanted to have a baby. His mom could not grow a baby in her belly because her belly was broken and this made them very sad.

One sunny day, they met a very nice lady named Jessica.
She was a surrogate. A surrogate is a special person
who carries a baby in their belly to help another family.

Jessica saw how sad Mikey's mom and dad were and thought,
"I would love to help!" Mikey was grown in Jessica's belly.
Jessica and Mikey's parents became great friends.

He, just like the watermelon, was not grown at home. While Mikey was growing in Jessica's belly, his parents' love for him was quickly growing in their hearts.

Mikey was very happy to grow his special watermelons in his grandmother's garden.

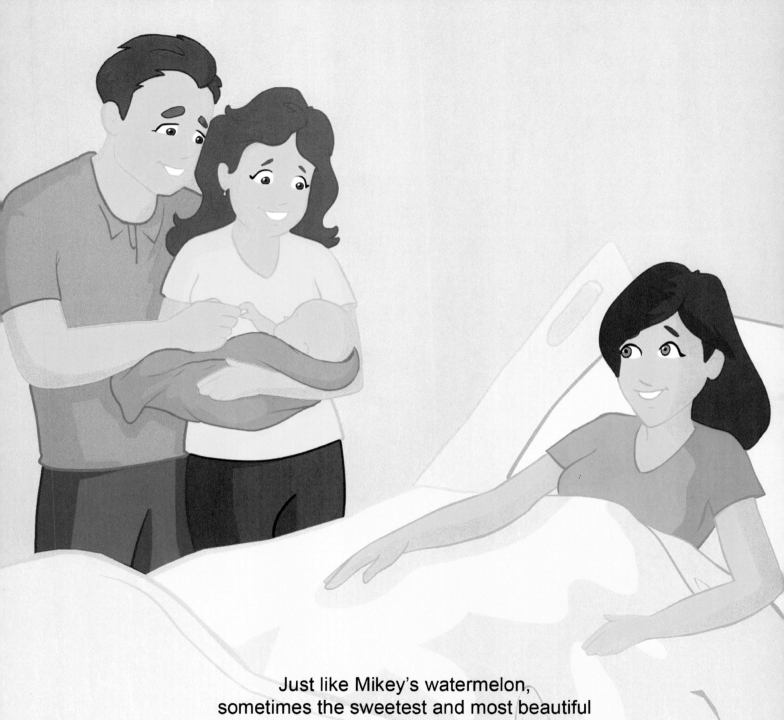

Just like Mikey's watermelon,
sometimes the sweetest and most beautiful
creations are grown in another garden.

Now faith is the assurance of things hoped for, the conviction of things not seen.

— Hebrews 11:1